# Celtic Mandolin

## by Andrew Driscoll

Online Audio  www.melbay.com/30036BCDEB

---

### Audio Contents

| | | | | |
|---|---|---|---|---|
| 1 | Cherish The Ladies | | 9 | Lady Jane Grey |
| 2 | Drowsy Maggie | | 10 | The Rocky Road to Dublin |
| 3 | The Shores of Galway Air | | 11 | Sandy Buchanan |
| 4 | Miss McLeod's Reel | | 12 | Kirkintilloch Waltz |
| 5 | Chorus Jig | | 13 | Smash the Windows |
| 6 | Red Eye Hornpipe | | 14 | Star of County Down |
| 7 | Stone Cutter's Jig | | 15 | Sixpence Strathspey and Reel |
| 8 | Fisherman Johnny's Reel | | 16 | Tivoli Jig |

---

1 2 3 4 5 6 7 8 9 0

**Visit us on the Web at www.melbay.com — E-mail us at email@melbay.com**

# Table of Contents

# Introduction

This book contains arrangements of traditional Celtic music as well as contemporary Celtic compositions for the mandolin. The style of the original music draws on both the Irish and Scottish traditions. Jigs, reels, strathespy, airs and contemporary forms are all represented. This book can be either a mandolinist's introduction to a variety of Celtic styles or a means to build repertoire for more experienced musicians.

# Before You Begin

The difficulty level of the material varies somewhat between the exercises as well as within the exercises themselves. Therefore, if you encounter something that is too difficult feel free to move on to another example. You can always return to the harder material later.

All of the examples are written in standard notation as well as mandolin tablature. All but the solo mandolin arrangements include the chordal part that is played on the recording. The chord symbols are included as well.

# Celtic Picking Patterns

Below are listed some recurring picking patterns that appear in Celtic styled music. Becoming familiar with them will make learning the material in the book easier. I would suggest that you practice them on all of the open strings. Then, you can practice crossing strings.

# Jig Patterns

Although you can play a double jig with straight alternate picking, the following pattern places the accents on the first and fourth beats naturally.

# Reel and Hornpipe Patterns

# Strathespy Pattern

# Mandolin Tuning

The examples in the book use the standard mandolin tuning. You can use the chart below along with a tuner or piano to tune your instrument.

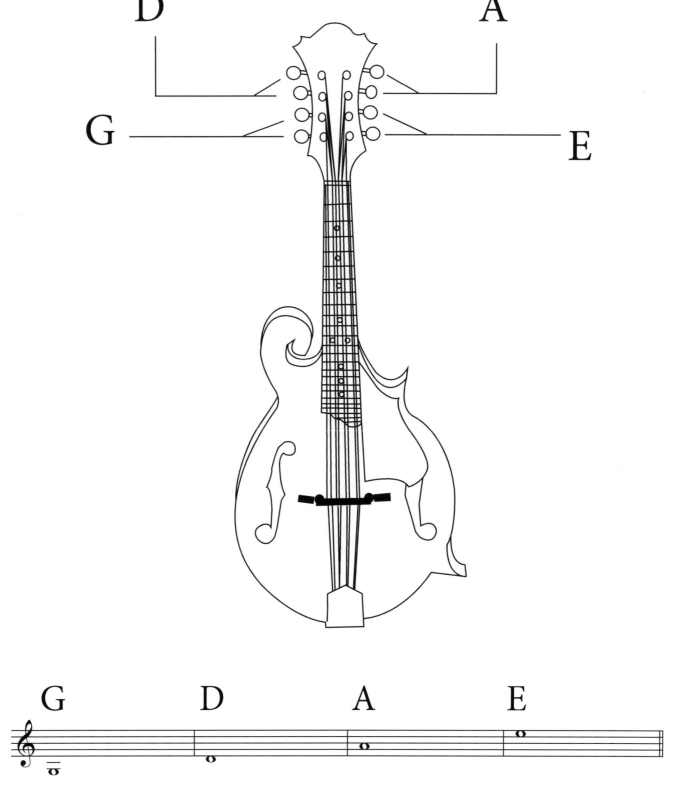

# Mandolin Fingerboard Chart

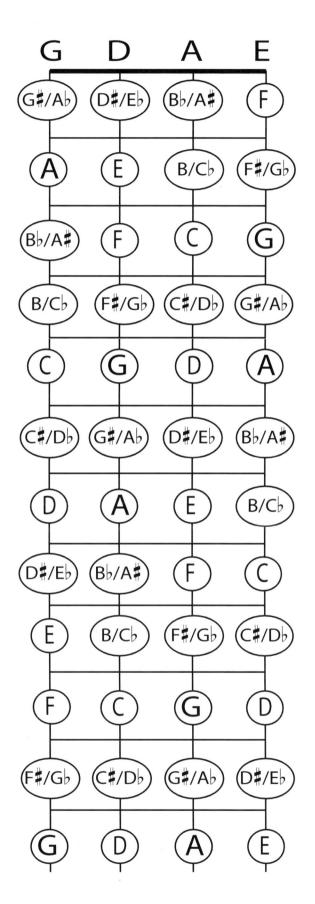

# Cherish The Ladies

Traditional

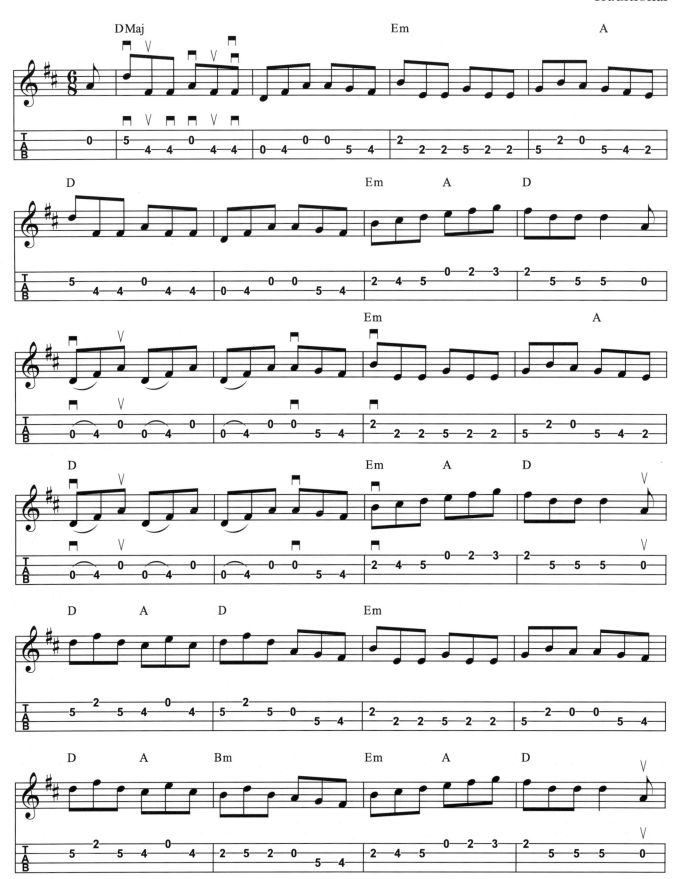

# Cherish The Ladies Chords

Traditional

13

# Drowsy Maggie

Traditional

# Drowsy Maggie Chords

Traditional

# The Shores of Galway Air

Andrew Driscoll

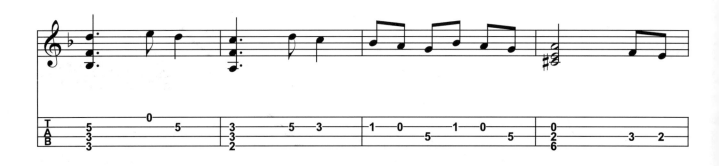

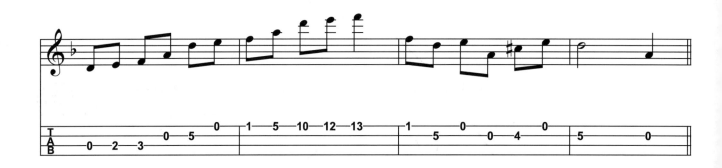

17

# Miss McLeod's Reel

Traditional

# Miss McLeod's Reel Chords

Traditional

# Chorus Jig

Traditional

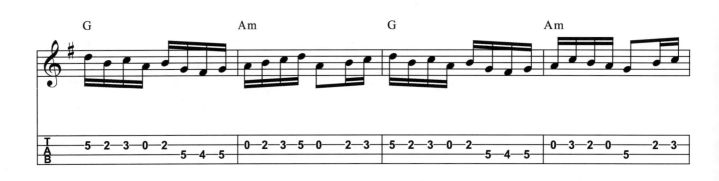

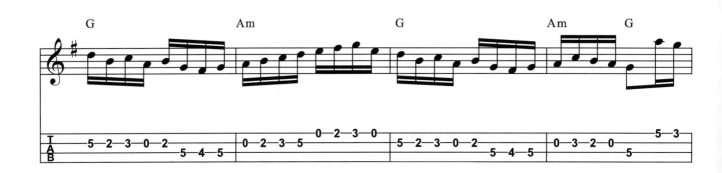

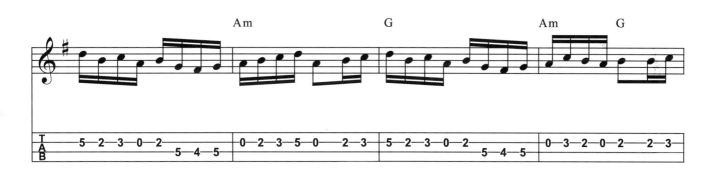

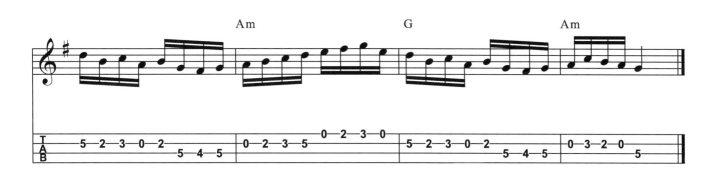

# Chorus Jig Chords

Traditional

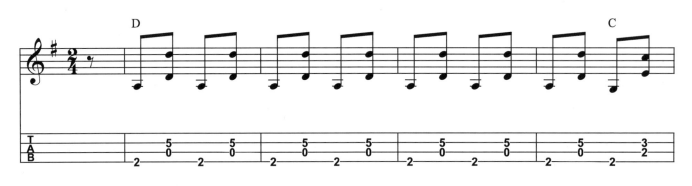

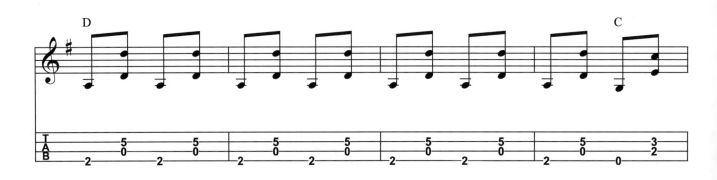

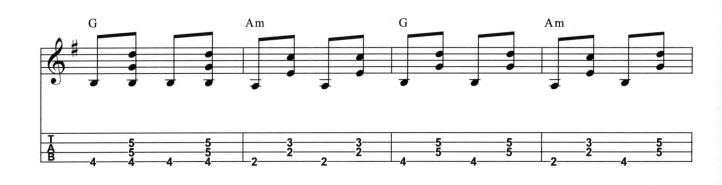

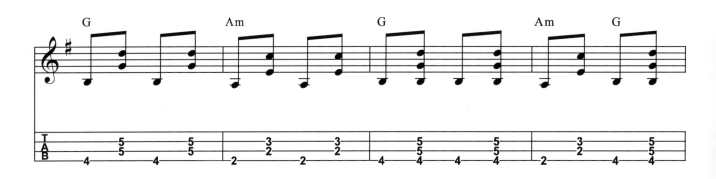

# Red Eye Hornpipe

Andrew Driscoll

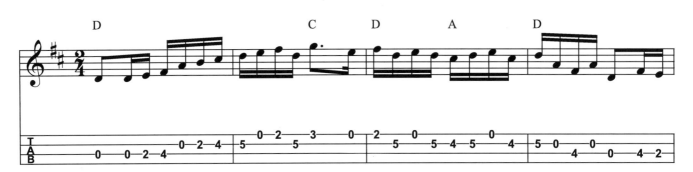

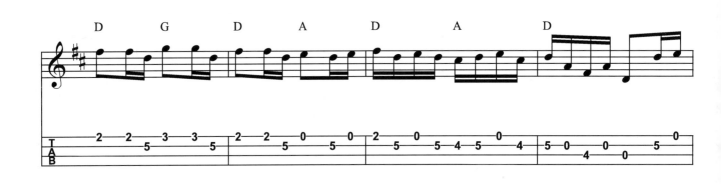

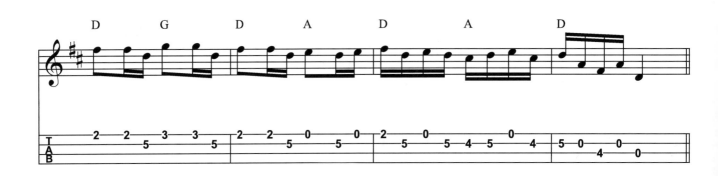

# Red Eye Hornpipe Chords

Andrew Driscoll

# Stone Cutter's Jig

Andrew Driscoll

# Stone Cutter's Jig Chords

Andrew Driscoll

# Fisherman Johnny's Reel

Andrew Driscoll

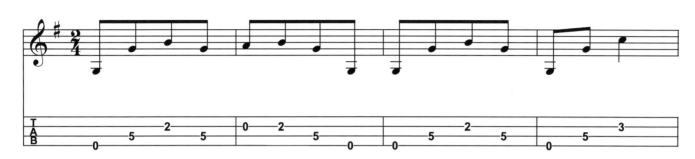

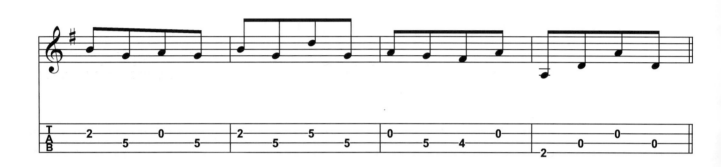

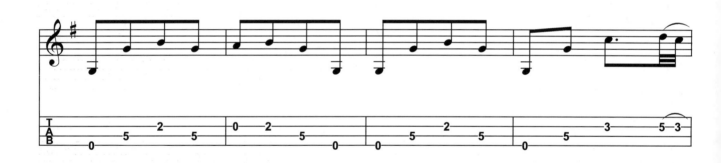

This page has been left blank
to avoid awkward page turns.

# Lady Jane Grey

Traditional

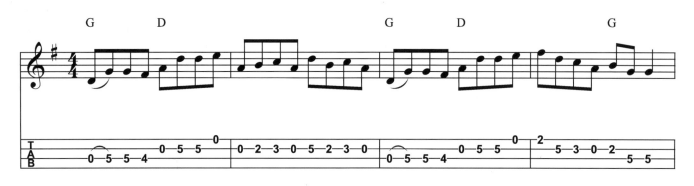

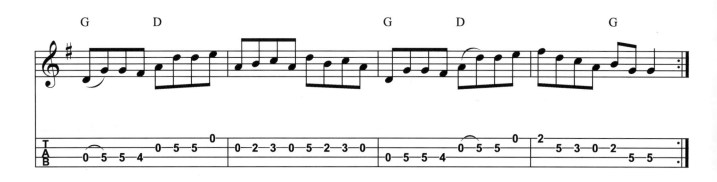

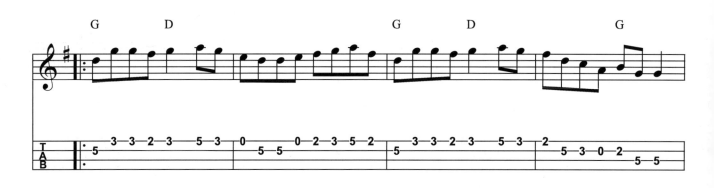

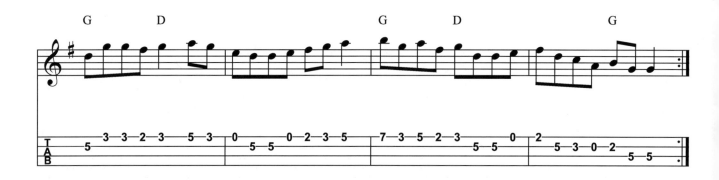

This page has been left blank
to avoid awkward page turns.

# Lady Jane Grey Chords

Traditional

# The Rocky Road to Dublin

Traditional

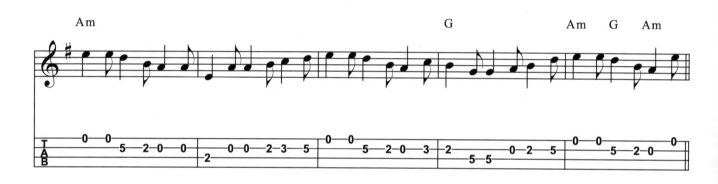

# The Rocky Road to Dublin Chords

Traditional

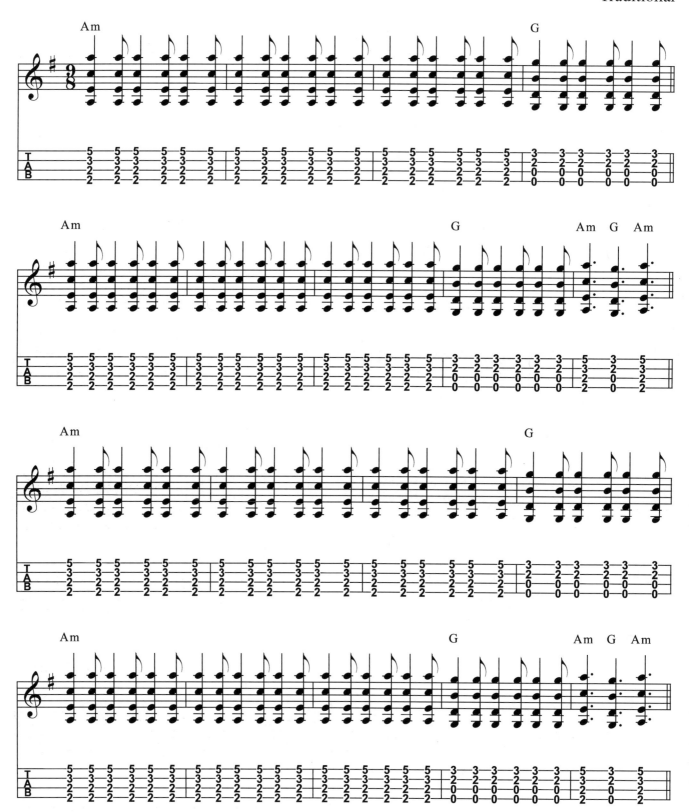

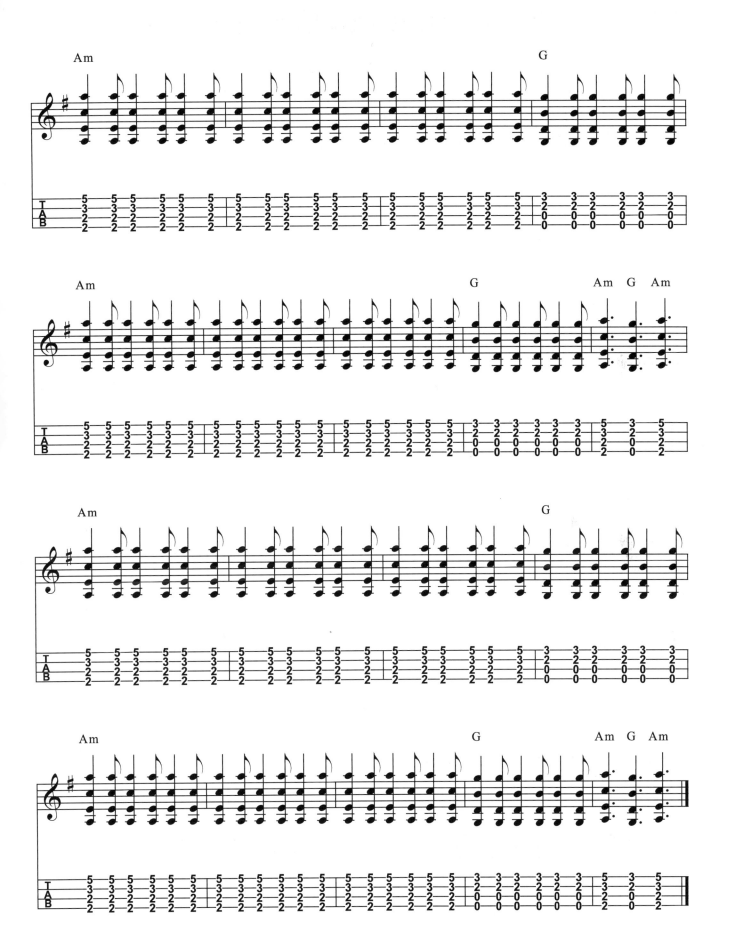

# Sandy Buchanan

Traditional

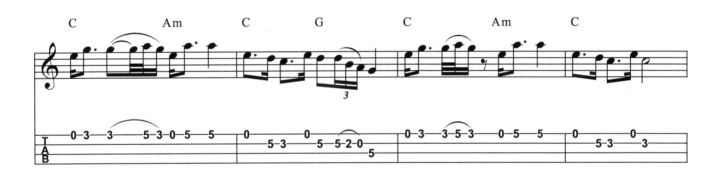

Track 11

# Sandy Buchanan Chords

Traditional

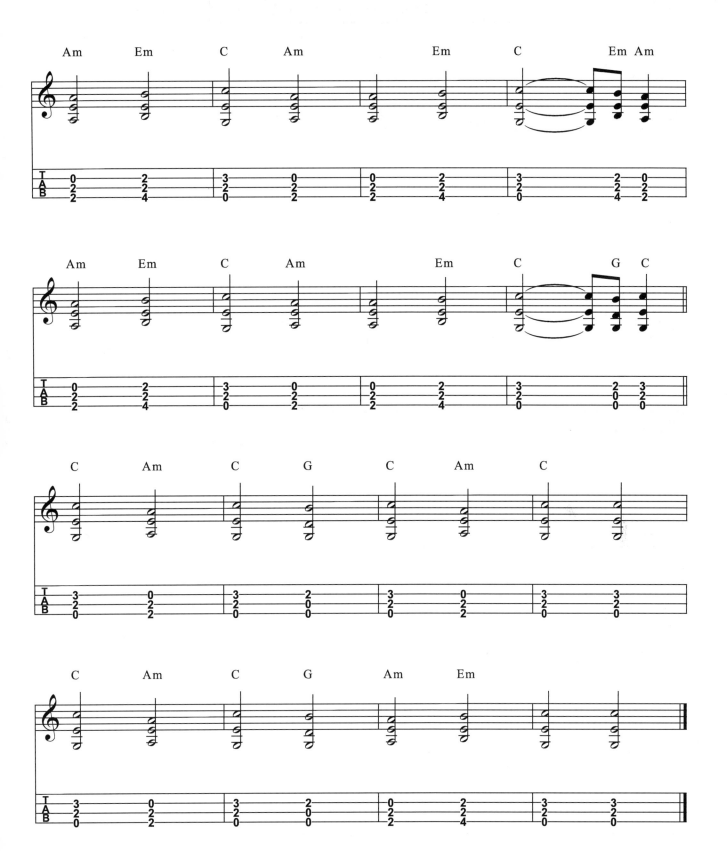

# Kirkintilloch Waltz

Andrew Driscoll

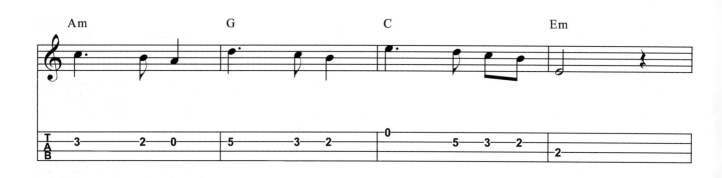

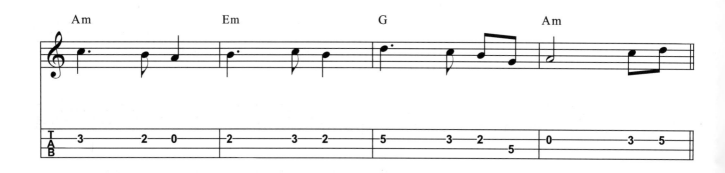

# Kirkintilloch Waltz Chords

Andrew Driscoll

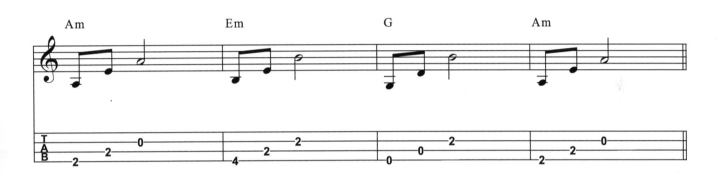

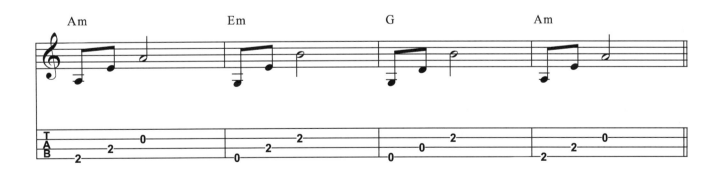

# Smash the Windows

Traditional

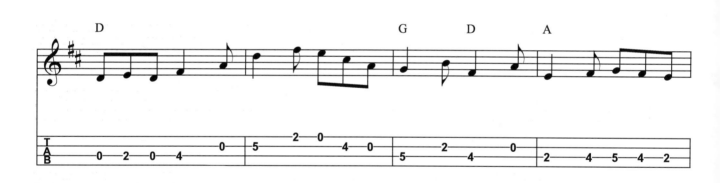

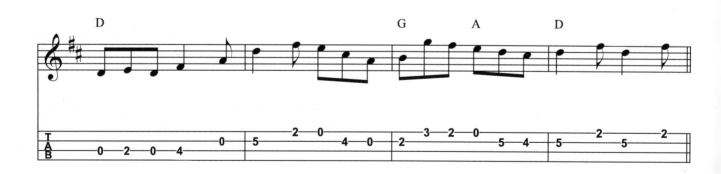

# Smash the Windows Chords

Traditional

# Star of County Down

Traditional

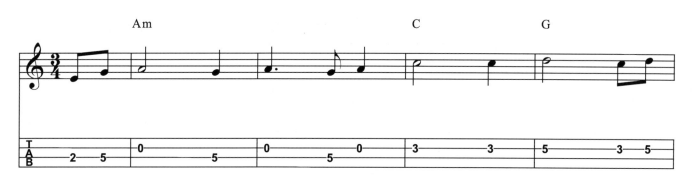

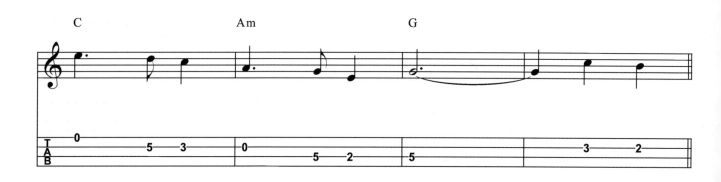

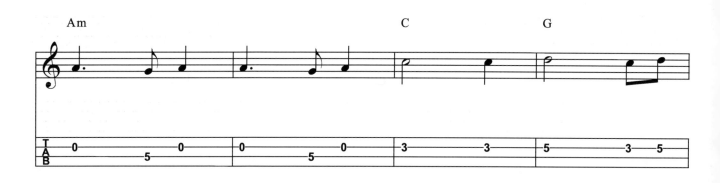

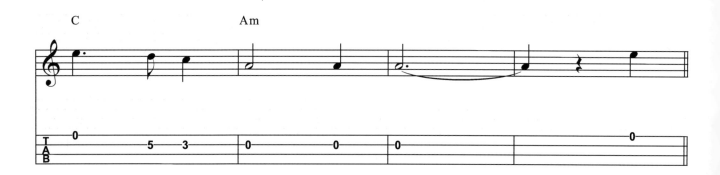

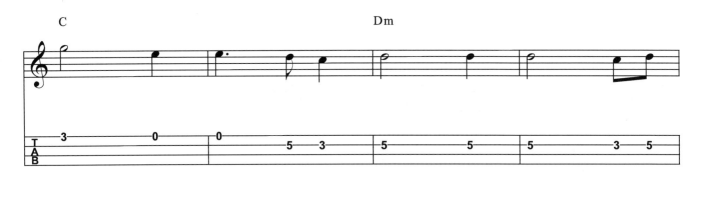

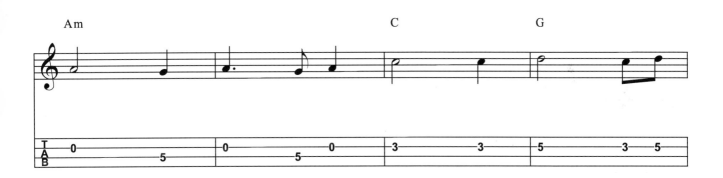

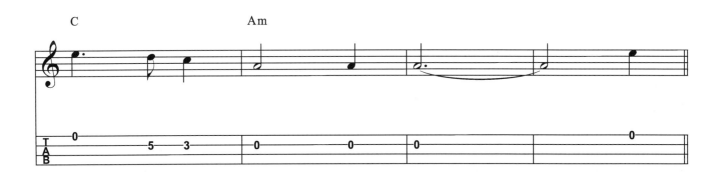

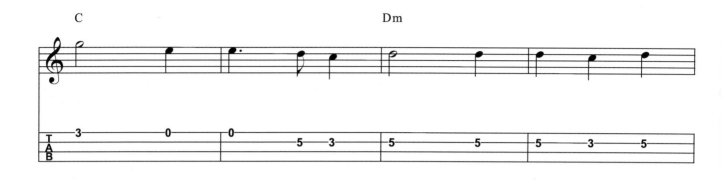

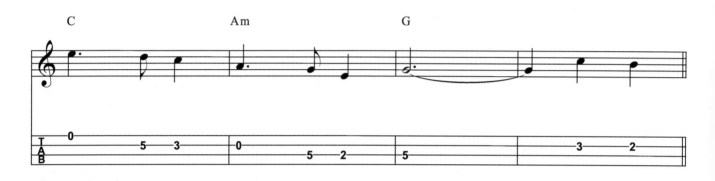

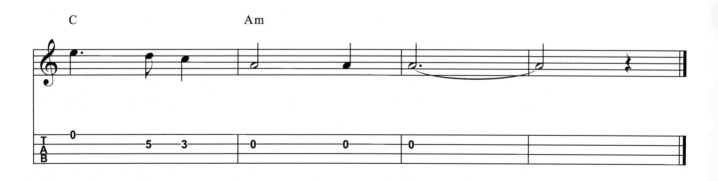

# Star of County Down Chords

Traditional

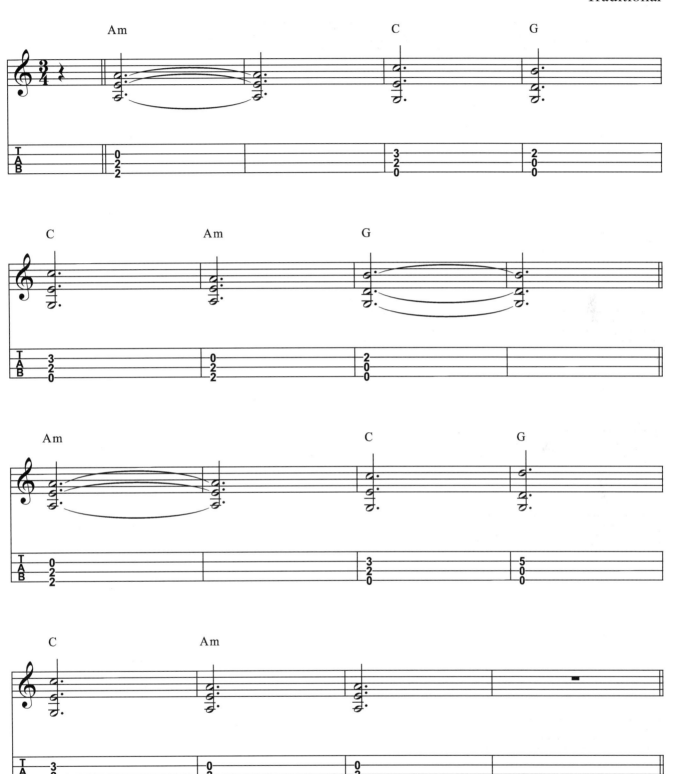

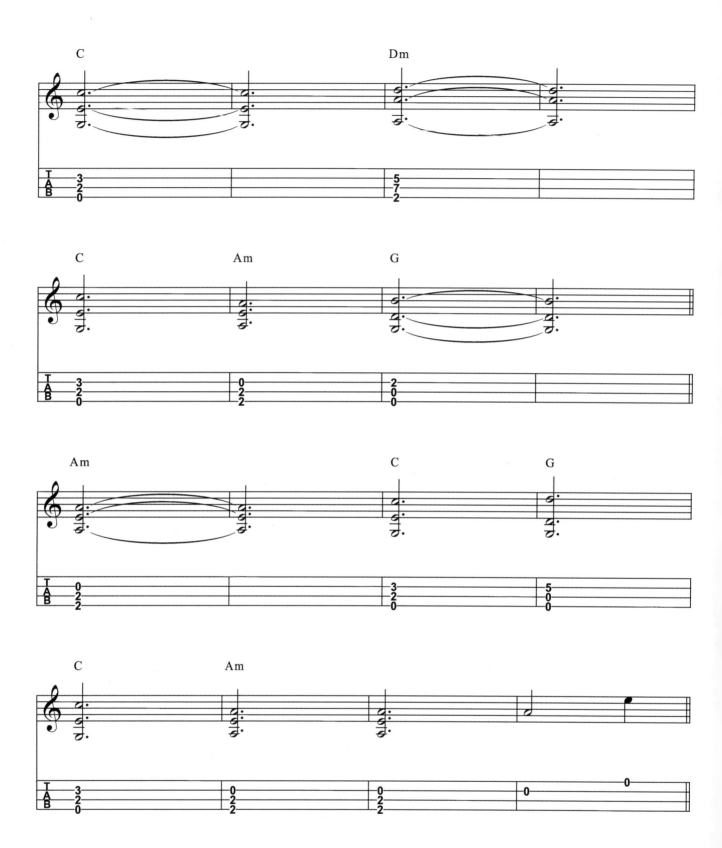

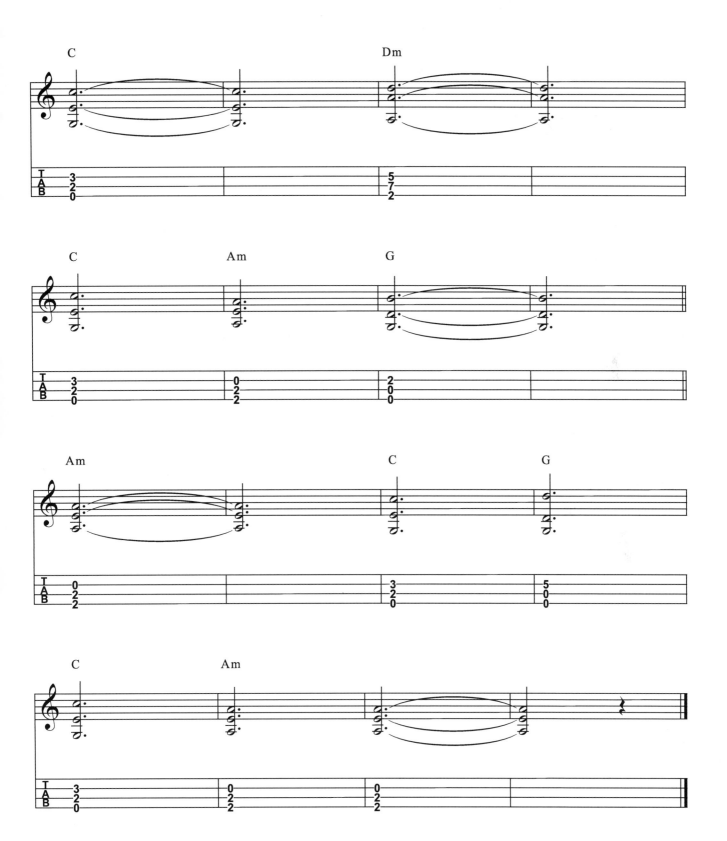

# Sixpence Strathspey and Reel

Andrew Driscoll

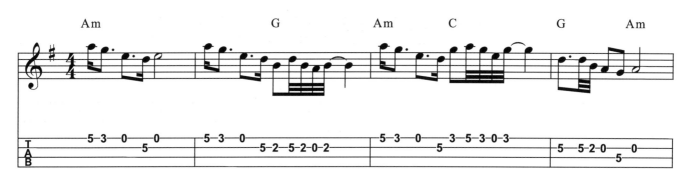

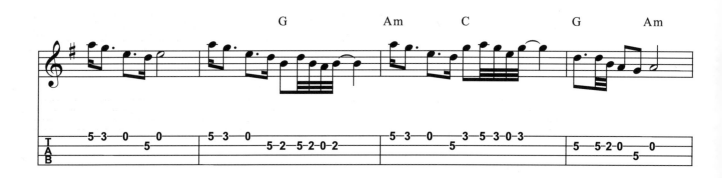

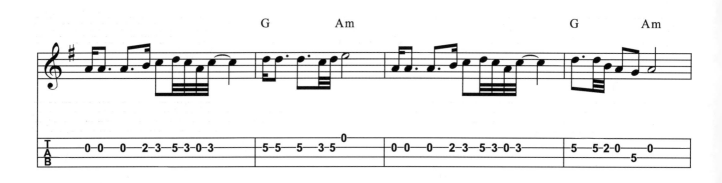

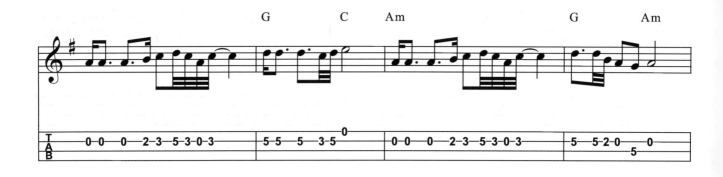

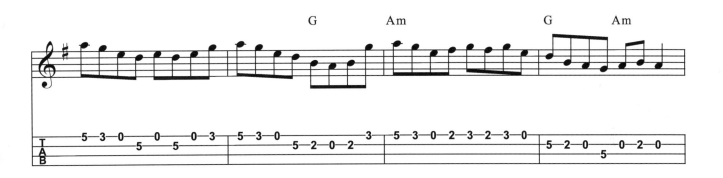

# Sixpence Strathspey and Reel Chords

Andrew Driscoll

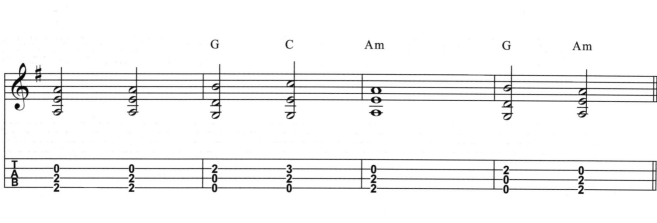

# Tivoli Jig

Andrew Driscoll

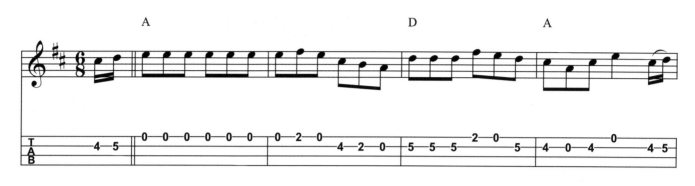

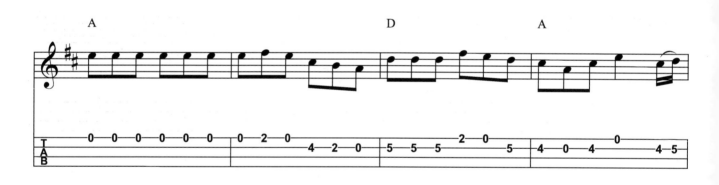

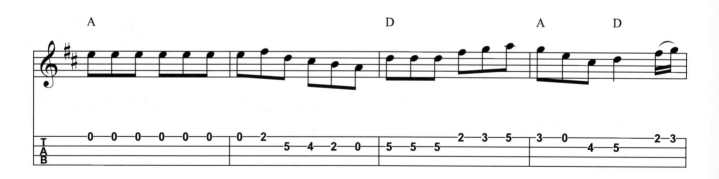

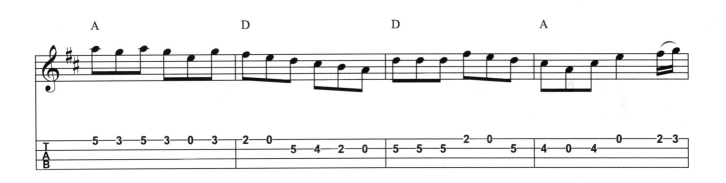

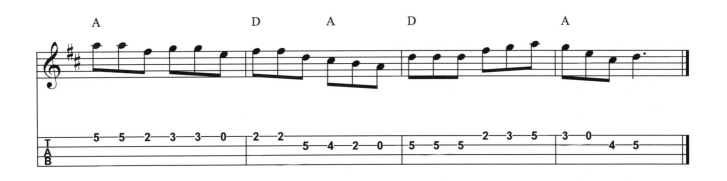

# Tivoli Jig Chords

Andrew Driscoll

# Notes

# Notes

Manufactured by Amazon.ca
Bolton, ON